GW00420585

For my very dear Friend

With calming thoughts from

Other books in this series:

Best Friends
Thank you Mum
Have a Perfect Day
My Dad, My Hero
I've got a crush on you

Published in 2010 by Helen Exley Giftbooks in Great Britain. A copy of the CIP da
is available from the British Library on request. All rights reserved. No part of this
publication may be reproduced or transmitted in any form or by any means,
electronic or mechanical, including photocopy, recording or any information stora
and retrieval system without permission in writing from the Publisher.
Printed in China.

Words and illustrations © Jenny Kempe 2010
Design and arrangement © Exley Publications 2010
The moral right of the author has been asserted.

12 11 10 9 8 7 6 5 4 3

ISBN: 978-1-84634-492-3

Dedication: To Keiran, with love.

Published by HELEN EXLEY®
Helen Exley Giftbooks, 16 Chalk Hill, Watford, Herts WD19 4BG,
www.helenexleygiftbooks.com

Stay Calm

WORDS AND ILLUSTRATIONS BY

JENNY KEMPE

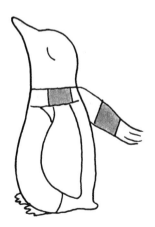

Take your time.

Reflect on the miracle of life.

Contemplate something
that is bigger
and more glorious
than yourself.

Let go of stress.

Enjoy being kind.

Surround yourself
with beautiful things.

Count your blessings.
They are all around you.

Be gentle.

Plan your day in advance.
Go about your work calmly,
one thing at a time.

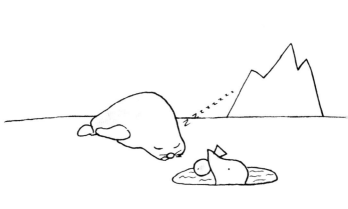

Pick one of your many projects.

Finish it.

Study the world
with new eyes.

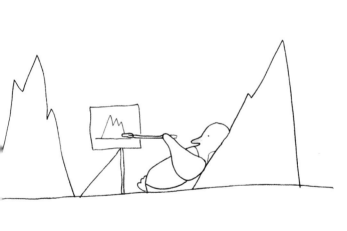

Let go of your anger.

Learn how to say no.

Spend your free tim

ɔing things *you* like.

Enjoy the moment.

Stay warm.

Quiet.

Breathe

Jenny Kempe

In 2009, overwhelmed by the endless bad news in the media, Jenny Kempe decided to take a six month break from newspapers, TV and radio. She turned her focus to the things in life that made her happy; to friends and family and to "taking time to just be". The result is the wonderfully bright and positive gift book series "Life is Beautiful". Each title has been designed to warm your heart and to put a smile on your face. As gifts, these books will brighten up the day, or even the life, of someone you care for.

About Helen Exley gifts

Helen Exley products cover the most powerful range of all
human relationships: love between couples, the bonds within
families and between friends. No expense is spared in making
sure that each book is as thoughtful and meaningful a gift
as it is possible to create: good to give, good to receive.
You have the result in your hands. If you have loved it –
tell others!

**Visit our website to see all of Helen Exley's other books
and gifts: www.helenexleygiftbooks.com**

Helen Exley Giftbooks
16 Chalk Hill, Watford, Herts
WD19 4BG, UK
www.helenexleygiftbooks.com

We loved making this book for you.
We hope you'll enjoy the other titles
in our series Life is Beautiful.

The Life is Beautiful Team